Ecosystems

Oceans

by Nadia Higgins

Bullfrog Books

Ideas for Parents and Teachers

Bullfrog Books let children practice reading informational text at the earliest reading levels. Repetition, familiar words, and photo labels support early readers.

Before Reading

- Discuss the cover photo. What does it tell them?

- Look at the picture glossary together. Read and discuss the words.

Read the Book

- "Walk" through the book and look at the photos. Let the child ask questions. Point out the photo labels.

- Read the book to the child, or have him or her read independently.

After Reading

- Prompt the child to think more. Have you ever visited the ocean? Have you seen videos or pictures? How would you describe it?

Bullfrog Books are published by Jump!
5357 Penn Avenue South
Minneapolis, MN 55419
www.jumplibrary.com

Library of Congress Cataloging-in-Publication Data

Names: Higgins, Nadia, author.
Title: Oceans / by Nadia Higgins.
Description: Minneapolis, MN: Jump!, Inc., [2017]
Series: Ecosystems
"Bullfrog Books are published by Jump!"
Audience: Ages 5–8. | Audience: K to grade 3.
Includes index.
Identifiers: LCCN 2017000172 (print)
LCCN 2017002382 (ebook)
ISBN 9781620316801 (hardcover: alk. paper)
ISBN 9781620317334 (pbk.)
ISBN 9781624965579 (ebook)
Subjects: LCSH: Marine ecology—Juvenile literature.
Ocean—Juvenile literature.
Classification: LCC QH541.5.S3 H54 2017 (print)
LCC QH541.5.S3 (ebook) | DDC 577.7—dc23
LC record available at https://lccn.loc.gov/2017000172

Editor: Jenny Fretland VanVoorst
Book Designer: Molly Ballanger
Photo Researcher: Molly Ballanger

Photo Credits: Biosphoto: Mathieu Foulquié, 13; Fabien Michenet, 20–21. Getty: KEVIN A HORGAN/SCIENCE PHOTO LIBRARY, 6–7; _548901005677, 12. iStock: Hoatzinexp, 16. Shutterstock: Willyam Bradberry, cover, 4, 23br; Palokha Tetiana, 1; archana bhartia, 3; Seaphotoart, 5, 23tr; A7880S, 24. SuperStock: Water Rights, 8–9; Westend61, 10–11; Minden Pictures, 14–15; Peter Verhoog/Buitenbeeld/Minden Pictures, 17; Flip Nicklin/Minden Pictures, 18–19.

Printed in the United States of America at Corporate Graphics in North Mankato, Minnesota.

Table of Contents

Above and Below 4

Where Are the Oceans? 22

Picture Glossary 23

Index 24

To Learn More 24

Above and Below

On the surface, waves sparkle and crash.

Animals swim below.
This is the ocean.

ocean

Oceans cover
most of Earth.

The water is salty.

It is deep.

Oceans are full of life.

Tiny plants float on top.

They need sunlight.

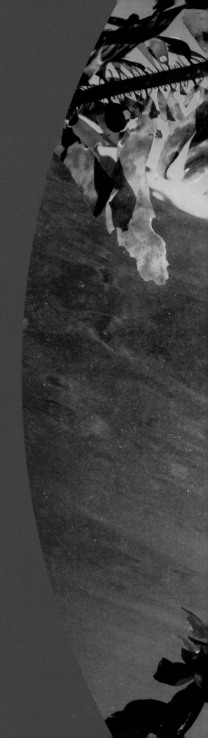

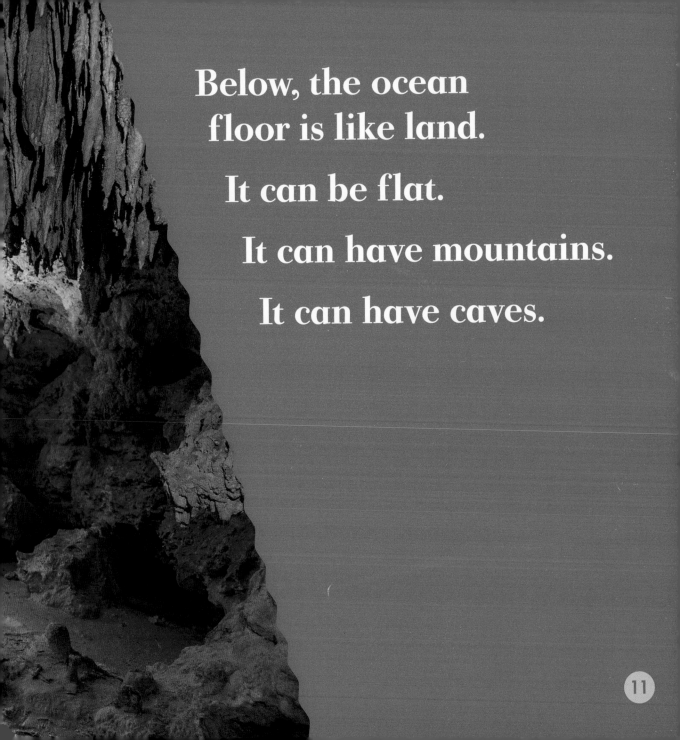

Below, the ocean
floor is like land.

It can be flat.

It can have mountains.

It can have caves.

Sea grass grows there.
Small fish eat the grass.

sea grass

12

Bigger animals eat the fish.

13

flipper

Sea animals
sure can swim.

Look!

A turtle flaps
its flippers.

15

A shark waves its tail.

The shark does not need air.

It has gills.

It gets oxygen from water.

gills ····▶

A whale needs air.

Whoosh!

It comes up for a breath.

Then it sinks back under the waves.

Where Are the Oceans?

The five oceans of the world are actually connected in one continuous body of water.

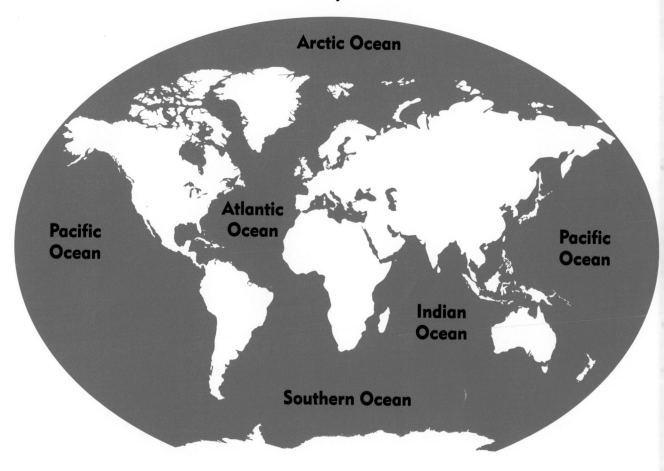

Arctic Ocean

Pacific Ocean

Atlantic Ocean

Pacific Ocean

Indian Ocean

Southern Ocean

■ ocean

Picture Glossary

flippers
Wide, flat body parts that turtles, seals, and other animals use to swim.

ocean floor
The bottom of the ocean.

gills
A body part that fish and some other animals use to take oxygen from water.

oxygen
A gas in air and water that animals need to live.

Index

air 17, 19

animals 5, 13, 15

caves 11

fish 12, 13

grass 12

mountains 11

plants 8

salty 7

shark 16, 17

turtle 15

waves 4, 20

whale 19

To Learn More

Learning more is as easy as 1, 2, 3.

1) Go to www.factsurfer.com

2) Enter "oceans" into the search box.

3) Click the "Surf" button to see a list of websites.

With factsurfer.com, finding more information is just a click away.